D1757530

Windsor and Maidenhead

95800000206291

What Did
JESUS
Do?

An introduction to the life and teachings of Jesus

Deborah Lock

LION
CHILDREN'S

Text by Deborah Lock based on text from *Tell Me About Jesus* (2006) by Lois Rock
This edition copyright © 2021 Lion Hudson IP Limited

All rights reserved. No part of this publication may be reproduced or transmitted in any form or by any means, electronic or mechanical, including photocopy, recording, or any information storage and retrieval system, without permission in writing from the publisher.

Published by
Lion Hudson Limited
Prama House, 267 Banbury Road
Summertown, Oxford OX2 7HT, England
www.lionhudson.com

ISBN 978 0 7459 7967 0
First edition 2021

Acknowledgments
The publisher would like to thank Claire Clinton, Director of Religious Education and RSHE, RE Matters Ltd for consultancy advice.
Scripture quotations marked GNB are taken from the Good News Bible © 1994 published by the Bible Societies/HarperCollins Publishers Ltd UK, Good News Bible© American Bible Society 1966, 1971, 1976, 1992. Used with permission.

Picture acknowledgements
Every effort has been made to contact the illustrators of this work, although this has not been possible in all cases. If notified, the publisher will rectify any errors or omissions at the earliest opportunity.

Illustrations
Alan Parry: pp. 7, 29; **Carolyn Cox**: pp. 1, 5, 8, 10, 11, 12 and front cover, 14, 17, 18, 21, 22, 24, 25, 27, 30, 31, 32, 34, 38, 40, 42 and back cover (from *The Lion Children's Bible*); **Gail Newey**: pp. 15(r), 16, 19, 20, 28, 45; **Lion Hudson IP Ltd**: (Jacqui Crawford) pp. 4, 13, 43; (John Williams) p. 39; **Rex Nicholls**: p. 33; **Richard Scott**: pp. 6, 26, 36, 37

Photographs
Alamy: p. 23 (Travelpix); p.35 (Godong); **istock**: pp. 9, 15(l) (INchendio); **Shutterstock**: p. 41 (MyraMyra)

A catalogue record for this book is available from the British Library

Printed and bound in China, July 2021, LH54

CONTENTS

Where did Jesus LIVE?

Jesus is the person whose life and teachings are central to the Christian faith. He lived 2,000 years ago in an area on the eastern coast of the Mediterranean Sea. At this time, the **Romans** ruled the **land** as part of their **empire**. However, the **Jewish people**, who lived in this area, were able to follow their own faith and traditions. Jesus was born into the Jewish faith.

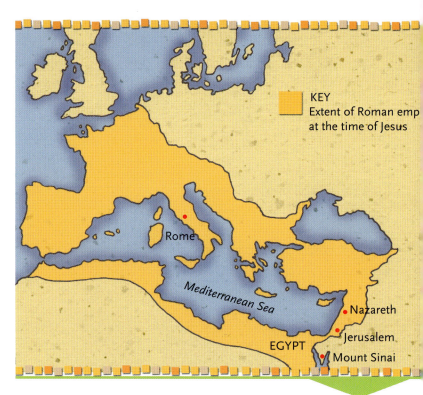

KEY
Extent of Roman emp
at the time of Jesus

Rome

Mediterranean Sea

Nazareth

Jerusalem

EGYPT

Mount Sinai

Jesus spent most of his life around Nazareth. Jerusalem was the most important place for the Jewish people.

The Jewish people

The history of the Jewish people began with a man named Abraham. They believed that God had promised him that he would be the father of a great nation. This nation would bring God's blessing to the world. Abraham's descendants faced hard times, but they were led out from slavery by a man named Moses. Through Moses, God made an agreement, or covenant, with the people. If they worshipped God and obey God's Laws, God would bless them and use them to bring about his purpose (or will) in the world.

The land of the Jews

The Jewish people settled in the land known as Canaan. Many generations passed before they defeated those nations who lived around them. They formed the kingdom of Israel and a king named David built a new city called Jerusalem. Afterwards the nation was divided and then defeated by other nations and empires. The people hoped that the words of their prophets about a new kingdom with a new king like David would come true.

The Roman empire

By the first century, the Roman empire had spread all around the Mediterranean Sea. The Romans put a king in place to govern the Jewish people. Roman soldiers were placed in the towns to keep order, and the people had to pay taxes to them. The Jewish people were able to have their own court, called the Sanhedrin, and there were two main Jewish religious groups called the Pharisees and the Sadducees.

Did you KNOW?

The Jewish people used the Hebrew word "Messiah" for God's promised king. The Greek word "Christ" has the same meaning.

Q: What language did Jesus speak?

Aramaic was the local language that Jesus would have spoken. The Jewish holy writings were written in Hebrew, so he would have learned this too. He may have also known some Greek, which was the language spoken throughout the Roman empire.

Jesus blesses the children.

How do we KNOW about Jesus?

People find out about Jesus from four books that were written about him. These are called the **Gospels**. They are found in the second section of the Christian Bible, known as the **New Testament**. The writers of the four books aim to share who they believe Jesus is, as God's Son and God's promised king.

The four Gospels

The life and teachings of Jesus are written about in four accounts known as the Gospels of Matthew, Mark, Luke, and John. It is likely that Mark's was the first to be written. Matthew and John are thought to have been written by two disciples, who knew Jesus. Luke was a doctor and was the only writer of the Gospels that was not Jewish. He became a follower of Jesus as the early church began.

The New Testament

The second part of the Christian Bible is called the New Testament. This is the writings of the first followers of Jesus. The word "testament" means a covenant or promise. This refers to the new covenant that Jesus explains to his followers, or disciples: God will forgive all sins through Jesus dying and raising to life so that all people can be with God for ever.

Did you KNOW?

The New Testament is written in Greek. There are 27 books in this part of the Christian Bible.

Luke was interested in Jesus' healings and also Jesus meeting with women and the Gentiles (non-Jews).

Q: What was the purpose of each Gospel?

The Gospel of Mark is the shortest and records the words and actions of Jesus. It begins: *This is the Good News about Jesus Christ, the Son of God.*

The Gospel of Matthew links the coming of Jesus to the fulfilment, or completion, of the Old Testament prophecies about a promised king sent by God, called the Messiah.

The Gospel of Luke aims to be an account in order of what happened in Jesus' life, to show Jesus as fully human and fully God.

The Gospel of John declares that Jesus is God, who from the beginning brought everything into existence. God came to live among people and show the glory of God. This is called incarnation.

The Gospel of John begins: In the beginning the Word already existed; the Word was with God, and the Word was God.

The Gospel of Matthew begins with a list of **Jesus' ancestors** and tells of the visit of the **wise men** after Jesus' birth. The Gospel uses the words of the **prophets** recorded in the Jewish Scriptures to show that they are now coming true. The writer aims to link Jesus as the awaited Messiah, God's promised king.

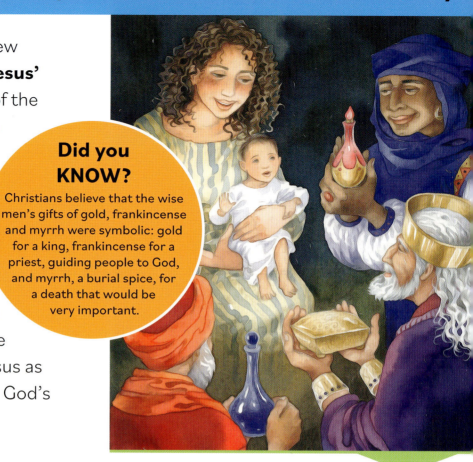

Did you KNOW?

Christians believe that the wise men's gifts of gold, frankincense and myrrh were symbolic: gold for a king, frankincense for a priest, guiding people to God, and myrrh, a burial spice, for a death that would be very important.

The wise men worshipped Jesus as the long-awaited king of the Jews.

Jesus' ancestors

The list begins with Abraham, the father of the Jewish people, and then names his descendants, leading to King David. From there the list continues with King David's descendants all the way to Joseph. Joseph is engaged to Mary. An angel visits him in a dream to tell him to marry her and to name her son, Jesus. The Jewish people believe that the Messiah will be a descendant of King David.

The wise men

The Gospel continues with the story of wise men, who saw a new star. They believed that this symbolized the birth of the king of the Jews. They journeyed from their own countries to find the new-born king and brought gifts to worship him. They first went to the Jewish city of Jerusalem where the ruling king, Herod, lived. After reading the scriptures, Herod sent them onto Bethlehem, ordering them to report back to him. They found Jesus and gave three unusual gifts. An angel warned them not to go back to Herod.

Q: What links were made to the Old Testament prophets?

The first part of the Bible is called the Old Testament and is made up of the Jewish holy writings. The Gospel of Matthew links their writings to events that happened at Jesus' birth.

The prophet Isaiah wrote:

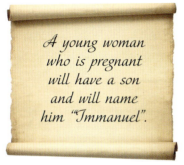

A young woman who is pregnant will have a son and will name him "Immanuel".

Jesus' mother, Mary, became pregnant because of a miracle of God.

The prophet Micah wrote:

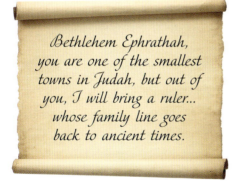

Bethlehem Ephrathah, you are one of the smallest towns in Judah, but out of you, I will bring a ruler... whose family line goes back to ancient times.

Jesus was born in the hilltop town of Bethlehem, the famous birthplace of King David.

The prophet Hosea wrote:

Out of Egypt I called my son.

After the wise men's visit, an angel appeared to Joseph warning that King Herod would hurt Jesus so they must flee to Egypt. They returned to Nazareth after Herod's death.

The prophet Jeremiah wrote:

A sound is heard in Ramah, the sound of bitter weeping. Rachel is crying for her children; she refuses to be comforted for they are dead.

On finding the wise men had not returned, Herod sent his soldiers to Bethlehem to kill all the young boys there.

What happened at Jesus' birth in LUKE's story?

The Gospel of Luke is the longest story of Jesus' growing up. This begins with the birth of **John the Baptist**, who would prepare people for the coming of Jesus. Then follows the story of **Mary**, chosen by God to be the mother of Jesus. Other events show that Jesus was someone very special.

Jesus was born in very humble surroundings.

The birth of John

The angel Gabriel appeared to a priest named Zechariah and said that he and his wife Elizabeth would have a son who would guide people back to God. This son was John and, when he was older, he told people to repent, saying sorry to God for their sins, and be ready for God's king. He baptized people with water in the River Jordan.

Mary's story

While Elizabeth was expecting her baby, something amazing happened to her cousin in Nazareth. Mary was engaged to be married to Joseph. She was visited by the angel Gabriel, who announced that God had chosen her to be the mother of a very special baby, Jesus. He would be called the Son of the Most High God.

The birth of Jesus

After marrying, Mary and Joseph had to travel to Joseph's family hometown to take part in a Roman census. Mary was due to give birth, but the town was crowded, so they found shelter with the animals. Mary's baby was born and she wrapped her child in swaddling clothes and laid him in a manger.

Q: What were signs that Jesus was very special?

Shepherds on the hillsides around Bethlehem were visited by angels announcing the birth of a saviour, Christ the Lord. They went to find Mary, Joseph, and the baby. Filled with joy, they believed the good news.

Mary and Joseph took baby Jesus to be presented at the Temple in Jerusalem, as was the Jewish custom. There they met two elderly people, Simeon and a prophetess named Anna. They both believed they were looking at the saviour of the people promised by God.

At the age of twelve, Jesus went to Jerusalem with his parents to celebrate the Jewish Passover festival. Afterwards his parents could not find him until they returned to the Temple and found Jesus talking with the wise teachers about the scriptures. The learned men were impressed by Jesus' wisdom and understanding.

Did you KNOW?

Each year, in some Christian churches, the four weeks leading up to Christmas are a time for preparing for Jesus' coming. This is called the season of Advent.

The teachers in the Temple were amazed at the boy Jesus' understanding of the Jewish Scriptures.

When did Jesus begin his MINISTRY?

When Jesus was about thirty years old, he began his **ministry** of teaching, healing, and guiding people to follow God. He began by being **baptized** and then prepared himself for forty days alone in the **wilderness**. He **toured** around for three years before he was put to death for proclaiming that he was God's promised king.

The baptism of Jesus is found in all four Gospels.

Jesus' baptism

Jesus began his ministry by being baptized by his cousin, John the Baptist. John preached that people needed to turn away from their wrongs against God (sins) and repent. He baptized those who repented by dipping them in the River Jordan.

When Jesus came to him, John was puzzled, for he believed Jesus had nothing to repent of. As John lifted Jesus out of the water, he saw the Holy Spirit of God come and settle on Jesus in the form of a dove. There was a voice from heaven saying: *You are my own dear Son. I am pleased with you.*

In the wilderness

After his baptism, Jesus went into the wild country for forty days. He fasted and prayed to prepare himself for what God was wanting him to do. The Bible says that he was visited by the Devil, who tested him and tried to tempt him away from God. Jesus resisted, replying with passages from the Jewish Scripture.

Did you KNOW?

In the forty days leading up to the most important Christian festival, Easter, many Christians prepare with prayer and self-denial, remembering Jesus' time in the wilderness. This is known as Lent.

Q: Where did Jesus travel?

Jesus spent much of his time in the area of Galilee. His hometown was Nazareth, but many of the events happened around the huge Lake Galilee, including in the town of Capernaum.

Many Jewish people did not enter the area of Samaria and journeyed on the other side of the River Jordan, but Jesus did travel through there for his ministry was for everyone.

The area of Judea was where Jesus was born in Bethlehem and died in the city of Jerusalem. The distance from Lake Galilee to Jerusalem was around 140 kilometres (87 miles).

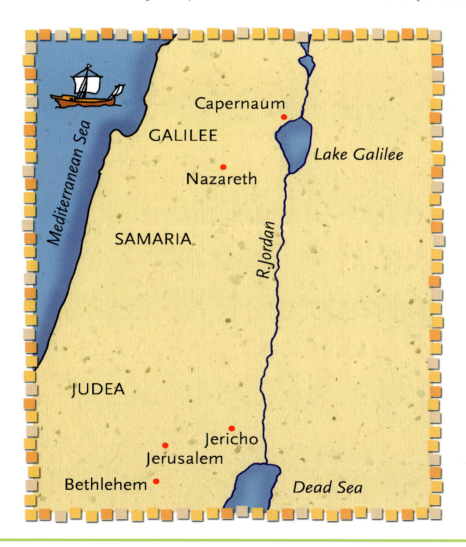

This map shows the most important places in the life of Jesus.

What was Jesus' MESSAGE?

Jesus' main message was about the **kingdom of God**. He spread the message that the kingdom of God was close at hand and beginning on earth with his ministry. Everyone could be part of the kingdom and receive God's blessings of hope, peace, and justice, if they lived as God's children. Jesus used stories called **parables** to explain his message.

The parable of the sower is told in the Gospels of Matthew and Mark.

The kingdom of God

Jesus message was about an everlasting kingdom where God reigns above all, and God's will is followed. The kingdom reflects God's vision for how people live perfectly with God. Jesus spoke about this kingdom as a precious gift from God. All people could belong by turning their lives around and following his example.

Spreading the message

Jesus spoke about his work and how people would receive his message like a man who went to sow a field, scattering handfuls of seed far and wide. Some seed fell on the path to be snatched away by birds. Some seed fell on rocky ground where they started to grow but then shrivelled, having no deep roots. Some seed grew up among thorns, choked by the worries of life. The seed that fell on good soil bore fruit, understanding the message.

Q: How did Jesus speak about the kingdom of God?

Sometimes called the kingdom of heaven, Jesus spoke about what the kingdom of God was like by using parables – stories that tried to help people understand that the kingdom exists in the lives and hearts of believers. These include the stories of:

- the man who, on finding the finest, most precious pearl, sells everything he had to buy it,
- a small mustard seed that grew into a tree where birds came and made their nests,
- the yeast mixed into bread dough to make it rise, and
- a net full of fish where good ones are kept, and worthless ones are thrown away.

Did you KNOW?

Jesus began his preaching in the synagogues, the places where Jewish people gathered for worship. In his hometown of Nazareth, an angry crowd threw him out after Jesus declared that a passage of Scripture was about himself:

The Spirit of the Lord is upon me, because he has chosen me to bring good news to the poor.
He has sent me to proclaim liberty to the captives
and recovery of sight to the blind,
to set free the oppressed
and announce that the time has come when the Lord will save his people.

Jesus used familiar sights and objects in his parables, such as a mustard plant, birds, a pearl, bread dough, and a fishing net.

What did Jesus TEACH?

Jesus taught that the kingdom of God exists in how people lived their lives as **God's children**. He explained that it was not enough to follow God's Law, but that they should strive to do the right thing even if this means hardship and danger. He told people how to turn away from their sins, the wrongs that separated them from God. He described what the **people of God's kingdom** were like.

Jesus told the crowds that they could show love to their enemies by carrying a soldier's pack twice as far as they had to.

Children of God

Jesus spoke of the kingdom belonging to those like children, who try to do the right thing with the help of God. Jesus told people to love their enemies and pray for those who hurt them, even the occupying Roman troops. He told people to turn the other cheek and not fight back. Jesus explained that the powerless, weak, and humble were great in the kingdom of God.

Turn away from sins

Jesus explained that some people would find it harder to enter the kingdom of God than others, as things of this world, such as pride and a love of money, would prevent them. Jesus told a rich young man that, to be perfect, he needed to sell all his possessions and give to the poor to receive treasure in heaven, and then come and follow him. As the young man went away sad, Jesus said: *It is much harder for a rich person to enter the kingdom of God than for a camel to go through the eye of a needle.*

Did you KNOW?

The phrase "the eye of a needle" is a metaphor for a narrow gap. The only way a camel could pass through such a gap is to have all its baggage removed and stoop down.

Jesus teaches his followers.

Q: What are people of God's kingdom like?

In the Gospel of Matthew, Jesus gives a sermon on a mountain to his followers. He describes the character of those who belong to God's kingdom and what they will receive. Each one begins with the word meaning "happy", "rich", or "blessed":

*Happy are those who know they are spiritually poor;
    the kingdom of heaven belongs to them!*

Happy are those who mourn; God will comfort them!

*Happy are those who are humble; they will receive what God
    has promised!*

*Happy are those whose greatest desire is to do what God
    requires; God will satisfy them fully!*

*Happy are those who are merciful to others; God will be
    merciful to them!*

Happy are the pure in heart; they will see God!

*Happy are those who work for peace; God will call
    them his children!*

*Happy are those who are persecuted because they do what
    God requires; the kingdom of heaven belongs to them!*

17

What did Jesus say about FORGIVENESS?

Jesus told people that if they own up and repent (say sorry) to God for their sins (wrongdoing) then God would lovingly and joyfully **forgive** them. Without the burden of sin, they would feel **transformed**, as if being born again. He explained that to receive **God's forgiveness**, people must be prepared to **forgive others**.

A man who could not walk was lowered by friends through a roof to the feet of Jesus. This story is told in the Gospel of Luke.

Transformed lives

Jesus showed that he had God's power to forgive sins when he healed people. The religious leaders believed that only God could do this. One day, when Jesus was teaching in a crowded house, some men made a hole in the roof and let down on ropes a man who could not walk. When Jesus saw how much faith they had, he said to the man: *Your sins are forgiven. Get up and walk.* The man got up at once and danced his way home, praising God.

Forgiving others

The disciple named Peter once asked Jesus how many times he should forgive someone who wronged him. Would seven times be enough to live God's way? Jesus replied: *"'No, not seven times,' answered Jesus, 'but seventy times seven'"*. By saying this, Jesus meant that people must always forgive those who have done wrong to them as holding onto resentment would affect their relationship with God.

Did you KNOW?

Jesus talked to a religious leader named Nicodemus about being "born again". This means a "spiritual" new beginning when becoming part of God's kingdom. Nicodemus came at night to talk with Jesus because he did not want to be seen.

Q: How did Jesus explain God's forgiveness?

Jesus helped people to understand God's love and forgiveness through stories called parables.

The parable of the lost son is about a son who leaves home with his share of his father's money. He spends it all and then takes a job looking after pigs. He decides to return home, say sorry, and ask his father to hire him as a servant. When he was still a long way off, his father sees him and runs to hug him and celebrates with a welcome party.

The parable of the lost sheep is about a good shepherd with 100 sheep. When one goes missing, the shepherd searches everywhere until he brings his lost sheep safely home. He joyfully celebrates with a party. Through this story, Jesus showed that there is joy in heaven when a wrongdoer turns back to God.

Jesus' story about a father forgiving his son provided a glimpse of God's unfailing love.

What did Jesus say about ACTIONS?

Jesus often used the **Jewish Scriptures** (holy writings) as the starting point for his teaching. He helped people to understand how to act in **the right way** that showed respect to God and respect to others. He told people that those who did good would **transform the world** with their shining example.

A high priest (with the breastplate) and a temple priest (in white) led the worship at the Temple in Jerusalem.

The Jewish Scriptures

One day, an expert of God's Law came to ask Jesus about how to receive eternal life. He wanted to test Jesus' understanding. Jesus replied: "What do the Scriptures say? How do you interpret them?" The man answered, *"Love the Lord your God with all your heart, with all your soul, with all your strength, and with all your mind",* and *"Love others as you love yourself".* Jesus replied that he was right and to go and do that.

The right way to live

Jesus used parables to help people understand how to be kind to one another. One parable is about a good Samaritan. In those days, the Jewish people did not like the people from the area of Samaria, who had different religious traditions. One day, a man was travelling from Jerusalem to Jericho, a well-known route. On the way, he was attacked by robbers. A Jewish temple priest came by, but hurried past on the other side of the road. A Jewish Levite, who helped in the Temple, also hurried by. A Samaritan, a foreigner in the land, stopped and bandaged the man's wounds, helped him onto his own donkey, and led him to an inn to take care of him. The next day, he paid the innkeeper to continue caring for the man. This story can be found in the Gospel of Luke.

Did you KNOW?

The temple priests were expected to help people worship God. The Pharisees were very proud of how they kept God's Law in every detail. Jesus often criticized them for not following God with a good heart.

Q: How would followers transform the world?

Jesus told his followers to do good for its own sake, not for public praise. Their shining example would be a beacon of hope in a selfish and cruel world. People would notice and they would praise and want to know God. In the Gospel of Matthew, Jesus says: *In the same way your light must shine before people, so that they will see the good things you do and praise your Father in heaven.*

Jesus shocked his audience by telling the parable of the good Samaritan, as the Samaritans were never viewed as good. But the story showed that living with a loving heart is more important than where people were born.

21

What did Jesus say about GOD?

Jesus talked about God as a **loving father**, who delights in caring and providing for his children and wants the best for them. He reminded people not to worry but trust in **God's goodness** and for answers to their prayers. He taught his followers to pray to God as **"Our Father"**.

Jesus prays with his disciples.

A loving father

When Jesus encouraged his followers to see God as a loving father or "daddy", this idea amazed them. From the Jewish Scriptures, God could seem like a frowning, critical judge who wanted to punish wrongdoers. Jesus explained to them that God was like a good parent taking care of his much-loved children, who will give good things to those who ask. He said: *Ask, and you will receive; seek, and you will find; knock, and the door will be opened to you.*

God's goodness

In the Gospel of Matthew, Jesus speaks about how God provides for the birds and dresses the flowers in loveliness, and asks the people: *Aren't you worth much more than birds?* He tells them not to worry about tomorrow but strive to do the right thing as part of God's kingdom and God will provide all they need.

Q: What are the words of the "Our Father" prayer?

Did you KNOW?

There is a church that stands on the place where Jesus is said to have taught his famous prayer. Panels around the walls give the words in 62 different languages.

These panels are on the walls of the Church of the Pater Noster in Jerusalem.

Jesus often went to pray, talk to God, especially before making any important decisions. He spoke about the importance of prayer as a way of praising God, asking God for his care and forgiveness, and praying for others, particularly those who wish to cause harm. When asked by his followers how they should pray in a meaningful way, Jesus taught them this prayer:

Our Father in heaven,
May your holy name be honoured;
may your kingdom come,
may your will be done on earth as it is in heaven.
Give us today the food we need.
Forgive us the wrongs we have done,
as we forgive the wrongs that others have done to us.
Do not bring us to hard testing,
but keep us safe from the Evil One.

What did Jesus' MIRACLES show?

The Gospels tell of many stories where Jesus worked **miracles**. These wondrous deeds showed people that Jesus had the **power of God** – power over illness, power over the natural world, and power to provide. This power for doing good was stronger than even death. These miracles brought joy and amazement.

At the Pool of Bethesada, Jesus healed a man who could not walk. This story is told in the Gospel of John.

Power over illness

Two thousand years ago, few people could afford good medical treatment, and many illnesses were not understood, so Jesus became famous for his miracles of healing. With just a touch, Jesus gave sight to people who could not see, made people walk again, and cured people who were sick from long-term illnesses. People who had been outcasts because of their wild behaviour, he healed so they were able to live normally again.

Power over death

When Jesus raised to life the young daughter of a man named Jairus, he told the family to keep this secret. Jesus' power over death was not shown to everyone until the death of his close friend Lazarus. Lazarus's body had been in a tomb for several days before Jesus arrived and asked for the stone door to be rolled away. Jesus called to Lazarus to come out and he came, still wrapped in the linen burial cloths. Many saw this wonder and believed Jesus to be God's promised king, the Messiah.

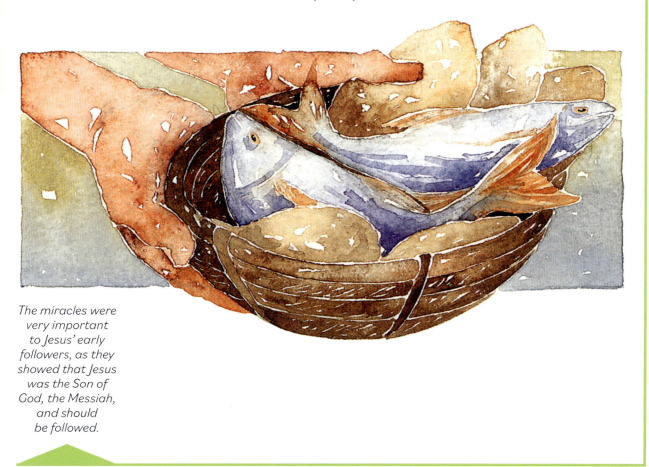

Did you KNOW?

Jesus worked miracles for non-Jews as well, such as the servant of a Roman centurion, showing that God's blessings were for all people.

Q: What are some of Jesus' other amazing miracles?

At a wedding in Cana, Jesus turned water into the best wine, so that the family would not have been ashamed of running out. This miracle is written in the Gospel of John.

With just five loaves and two fish, Jesus blessed and shared out the food, feeding a huge crowd of 5,000 people. The scraps that were gathered afterwards filled twelve baskets. This miracle is written in all four Gospels.

A violent storm blew up while Jesus and his disciples were on a boat crossing Lake Galilee. The terrified disciples woke Jesus, who simply stood up and commanded the wind and waves to be still. This miracle is written in the Gospels of Matthew, Mark, and Luke.

The miracles were very important to Jesus' early followers, as they showed that Jesus was the Son of God, the Messiah, and should be followed.

Who were Jesus' FRIENDS?

Jesus showed that he valued people for who they were, and not for their status, just as God did. All were welcomed to be part of God's kingdom, including **children**. As Jesus visited different places, he relied on **hospitality** from local people. He surprised the religious leaders that he chose to spend time with those they considered were sinners and **outcasts**.

Jesus at the home of Mary and Martha.

Jesus and the children

Jesus' close followers were slow to learn to be as welcoming as Jesus. One day, people came with their children and asked if Jesus would bless them. Jesus was busy healing many people. The disciples said they were wasting Jesus' time. But Jesus heard and stopped them, saying:

Let the children come to me and do not stop them, because the kingdom of God belongs to such as these.

Local hospitality

Local people offered Jesus and his close followers food and shelter as they toured around. In Bethany, a woman named Martha welcomed Jesus to stay in her home. She then busied herself with all the chores that had to be done. Her sister, Mary, simply sat and listened to Jesus' teaching. Martha was upset with Mary for not helping her, but Jesus explained to her that Mary had chosen to do what was best.

Did you KNOW?

Many Christian actions, including charities such as Christian Aid and Tearfund, are about treating everyone equally in the sight of God, serving the poor, and offering hospitality, welcome, and care to a community.

Q: Who were the outcasts?

In Jesus' time, some people were not accepted in Jewish society. These people included the poor and sick, criminals, and some women. Jesus had compassion and spent time with them, healing or guiding them to turn around their lives.

People particularly hated those who cheated, such as tax collectors, who often took more money in tax to keep for themselves. One tax collector, Zacchaeus, climbed a tree to see Jesus because he was a short man and could not see over the crowd. Jesus noticed him and shared a meal with him. Afterwards Zacchaeus paid back to the poor four times the amount he had taken.

The story of Zacchaeus meeting Jesus is told in the Gospel of Luke.

Who followed JESUS?

Crowds of people followed Jesus, eager to hear his teaching about the kingdom of God. Some promised to devote their lives to him, but Jesus warned them of the **commitment and cost** needed. Jesus knew he needed help with his work, and he sent out his followers to places ahead of him. Jesus chose twelve followers to be his closest **disciples**, or apostles.

Did you KNOW?

The word "disciple" means a pupil or follower, who helps to spread the ideas of their teacher or leader and commits to following their example.

A person needs to keep their eye on the job to plough in a straight line, just like following Jesus.

The first disciples

Among the first followers of Jesus were the fishermen, Simon Peter and Andrew. Jesus used their boat to speak to the crowds. Afterwards, Jesus sent them out to fish. The nets were so full of fish that other fishermen, James and John, came to help. Once they had brought the fish to shore, Jesus said: *Come with me, and I will teach you to catch people.* They immediately left their nets and followed him. There was enough fish caught to support their families for many years.

Commitment and cost

Many people wanted to follow Jesus, but not everyone was ready to do so. He warned them that they would have to leave their homes, comforts, and families to be fully committed. Jesus described a person who starts ploughing but keeps looking back so they cannot do a proper job. Jesus also warned that, as his followers, they could expect to face danger, even the danger of being executed by crucifixion (on a cross).

Q: What are some facts about the twelve apostles?

Jesus' apostles had ordinary lives before meeting Jesus. Most of them were put to death for following him.

Simon Peter, a fisherman and brother of Andrew. He could be quick to act and speak, but was full of courage. He is thought to have died on an upside-down cross.

Andrew, a fisherman, who was a disciple of John the Baptist before following Jesus. He is thought to have died on a diagonal cross.

James, a fisherman and brother of John. Jesus nicknamed them both "Sons of Thunder", as they were quick to anger. He is thought to have died by a sword.

John, a fisherman, who is thought to be one of the writers of the Gospels and the last book of the Bible, Revelation. He died in exile on the island of Patmos.

The other apostles are:

Philip, who brought his friend Bartholomew to meet Jesus.

Bartholomew, also known as Nathanael, who was known as an honest man.

Matthew, a tax collector from Capernaum. He is thought to be one of the writers of the Gospels.

Thomas, who only believed what he could see, so was known as "doubting Thomas".

James, son of Alphaeus.

Jude, also known as Thaddeus or Judas, son of James.

Simon, a member of the zealots, a political party.

Judas Iscariot, who is known for betraying Jesus.

Who is JESUS?

Jesus knew that he had a huge following, but that many people thought he was just another prophet, who spoke messages from God. The religious leaders mistrusted him. However, Jesus shared more about himself with his closest disciples, as the **Messiah**, as **God's Son**, and with **sayings** about what he offers his followers.

Messiah

Three of the four Gospels record the event when Jesus asks his closest disciples: *"What about you? Who do you say I am?"* Peter answered, *"You are the Messiah"*. The Messiah is the name given to God's promised king written about in the Jewish Scriptures, who would be sent by God to save the nation and all people. Jesus tells them not to say a word about this to anyone. He warned of hard times ahead, explaining that he will be put to death, but will rise again on the third day.

God's Son

Six days later, Jesus went with his disciples Peter, James, and John to the top of a high mountain. Suddenly, Jesus' face shone with a heavenly light and his clothes became shining white. Two prophets of olden times – Moses and Elijah – appeared and began to talk to Jesus. A cloud came down and hid everything, but the disciples heard a voice saying: *This is my own dear Son, with whom I am pleased, listen to him!* This event is known as the transfiguration.

The story of the transfiguration is told in the Gospels of Matthew, Mark, and Luke.

Did you KNOW?

The terms "Messiah" and "Christ" both mean "anointed one".

Q. What did Jesus say about himself?

In the Gospel of John, there are several sayings of Jesus, which begin with the words "I am". Each saying gives a glimpse of what his life and teaching offers his followers.

I am the bread of life. Those who come to me will never be hungry.

I am the light of the world. Whoever follows me will have the light of life and will never walk in darkness.

I am the gate. Those who come in by me will be saved; they will come in and go out and find pasture.

I am the good shepherd, who is willing to die for the sheep.

I am the resurrection and the life. Those who believe in me will live, even though they die.

I am the way, the truth, and the life.

I am the vine, and you are the branches.

Jesus is likened to a shepherd, who keeps all his sheep safe from harm – even the ones who go astray.

What happened in JERUSALEM?

The most important festival of the Jewish people was **Passover**. Every Jew wanted to go to the Temple of Jerusalem for the festival, including Jesus and his disciples. When Jesus entered the city riding on a donkey, the people **welcomed** him as God's promised king. Every day, Jesus preached at the **Temple**, and the religious leaders wanted to silence him.

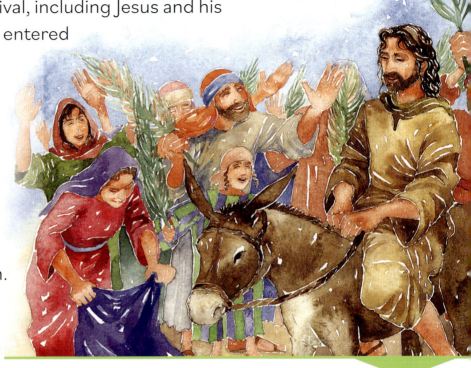

Festival of Passover

The Jewish festival of Passover remembers a key moment in their history, when God helped the Hebrews escape from being slaves in Egypt and made a covenant (a promise) to protect them. Each year, many Jews from all over the country would travel to the Temple in Jerusalem to purify themselves. They also ate and made an offering of a young lamb to God, as their ancestors had done on the night before their escape.

Welcomed as king

As Jesus approached the city, he asked his disciples to fetch a donkey so he could ride the last few miles. They joined the crowds going into the city, who recognized Jesus. They began to cheer and throw down their cloaks on the road, and wave palm branches, shouting: *Praise God! God bless him who comes in the name of the Lord. God bless the King of Israel!*

Christians remember Jesus' entry into Jerusalem on the Sunday before Easter, known as Palm Sunday.

In the Temple

When Jesus entered Jerusalem, he went to the Temple. The courtyard was like a marketplace where merchants were selling the special Temple coins needed for the right donations and doves and other animals for sacrifices. Jesus began to overturn the tables. He told the merchants that they had turned this "house of prayer" into "a den of robbers". Each day afterwards, people came to the Temple to be healed by Jesus and hear his teachings.

Q: Why did the religious leaders plot against Jesus?

The religious leaders mistrusted Jesus. They claimed he was disrespectful of God's Law, healing people on the Sabbath (the holy day of rest), and mixing with people who did wrong. They refused to believe his miracles showed that he had power from God. They were troubled by the huge crowds that followed Jesus, who were now welcoming him as the Messiah. They feared that he would stir up the people against them. They plotted to arrest him away from the crowds.

The Temple in Jerusalem was the focus of Jewish life and worship.

Did you KNOW?

One of Jesus' close disciples, Judas Iscariot, was paid thirty silver coins for letting the religious leaders know when Jesus could be arrested quietly.

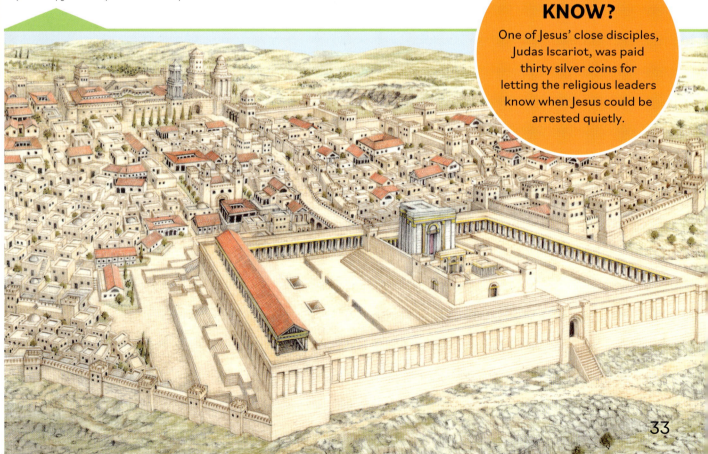

What happened at the LAST SUPPER?

Jesus and his disciples gathered in an upstairs room to share the **Passover meal**. Before eating, Jesus washed the feet of his disciples, giving them a **new commandment**. During the meal, Jesus began to explain the ceremony to his disciples in a new way, making God's **new covenant**. Jesus knew this was his last supper and warned his disciples of troubles ahead.

Jesus met with his closest disciples in the upper room of a house in Jerusalem.

The Passover meal

The Jewish Passover meal is full of ceremony and meaning to help remember the first Passover night. The traditional food includes matzoh, unleavened bread, as the Hebrew slaves left Egypt in a hurry, leaving no time for the dough to rise. The four cups of wine represent the covenant (promise) that was made between God and the Hebrews for being rescued, saved, and set free as God's chosen people.

The new covenant

During the Passover meal, Jesus gave new meaning to the sharing of the bread and the wine with his disciples. The Gospel of Luke describes the event: *Then he took a piece of bread, gave thanks to God, broke it, and gave it to them, saying, "This is my body, which is given for you. Do this in memory of me." In the same way, he gave them the cup after the supper, saying, "This cup is God's new covenant sealed with my blood, which is poured out for you".* The disciples did not understand the importance of what Jesus was saying about a new covenant at that moment.

Did you KNOW?

Since the first days of the Christian faith, believers have remembered Jesus by sharing bread and wine. This ceremony is known by many names, including Holy Communion, Mass, Eucharist, and the Lord's Supper.

Q: What was the new commandment?

The Gospel of John adds another detail about the last supper. Before the meal, Jesus tied a towel around himself and began washing the feet of his disciples as a servant would do. After doing this, he explained that he was setting them an example to serve one another like this. After the meal he gave them a new instruction to follow, saying: *Love one another. As I have loved you, so you must love one another.*

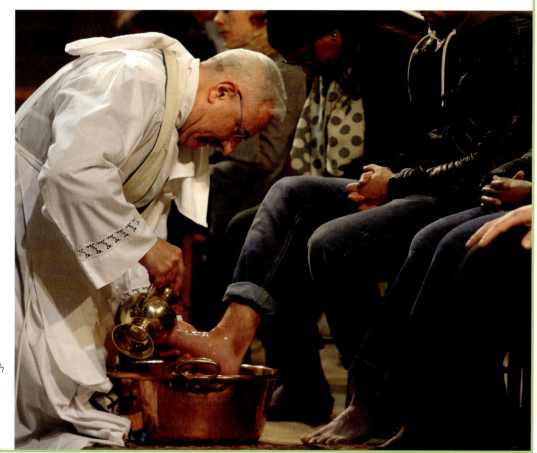

Some Christians still continue the tradition of foot washing in church services, often on the Thursday before Easter.

What happened at Jesus' TRIAL?

After the Passover meal, Jesus went with the disciples to the **Garden of Gethsemane**. After a night of prayer, Judas came and betrayed Jesus with a kiss. Jesus was arrested. Most of Jesus' disciples fled; Peter followed but denied knowing Jesus. Jesus was first tried by the **Jewish Council** then taken before the Roman governor, **Pontius Pilate**, to approve his punishment of death.

Temple guards arrested Jesus on the Mount of Olives, a hillside overlooking Jerusalem.

The Garden of Gethsemane

Outside Jerusalem was a hillside with a quiet olive grove known as the Garden of Gethsemane. There, Jesus prayed to God while his disciples slept. He knew that his enemies wanted to kill him. He desperately prayed for an easier way, but he knew that he must obey God to the end. Then came the crowd of armed men led by Judas. Judas gave Jesus a kiss on the cheek, as was custom for a greeting. Jesus was arrested and his disciples ran away frightened.

The Jewish Council

Jesus was taken to the house of the high priest, who was the head of the Sanhedrin. This was a council of chief priests and elders, who acted as judges over Jewish laws and issues. They all met to question Jesus. Jesus explained that everything he had done was known for he had taught openly. The high priest asked: *"Tell us if you are the Messiah, the Son of God?"* Jesus answered him, *"So you say. But I tell all of you: from this time on you will see the Son of Man sitting at the right side of the Almighty and coming on the clouds of heaven!"*

Jesus was accused of blasphemy – using the name of God in the wrong way. The punishment for this was death.

Did you KNOW?

Peter had promised to not desert Jesus. In the courtyard of the high priest's house, he sat among the servants. Some accused him of being a follower of Jesus. Three times Peter said that he did not know Jesus. Then a cock crowed. He remembered Jesus had predicted his denial and wept.

Q: Why did Pontius Pilate agree to Jesus' death?

The religious leaders took Jesus to Pontius Pilate, the Roman governor in Jerusalem. They needed him to approve Jesus' punishment of death. They accused Jesus of stirring up trouble and calling himself king. Pilate questioned Jesus, but he stayed quiet. Pilate was puzzled and found no reason why Jesus should die. The religious leaders told Pilate: *If you set him free, that means that you are not the Emperor's friend! Anyone who claims to be a king is a rebel against the Emperor!* They also stirred up the crowds, who gathered outside and shouted: "Crucify him!" It is thought Pilate agreed to put Jesus to death because he was afraid of a riot and afraid of losing his position.

A custom at the Passover festival was for the crowd to choose a prisoner to release. Pilate asked the crowd who they wished to release – Jesus or a criminal named Barabbas. The crowd chose Barabbas.

What happened at Jesus' CRUCIFIXION?

Now in the hands of the Roman soldiers, Jesus was **mocked as king** and then led through the streets of Jerusalem, carrying his cross. Jesus was **crucified** with criminals. He prayed as he hung on the cross. After he died, Jesus' body was laid in a new tomb with a stone door.

Jesus was crucified on a hill called Golgotha.

Did you KNOW?

Christians solemnly remember the day of Jesus' crucifixion as "Good Friday". They reflect on how Jesus suffered although he was innocent. The day is called "good" because they believe Jesus took on all the world's sins as an offering to rescue, save, and set free all people.

Mocked as king

For cruel fun, the Roman soldiers stripped Jesus and dressed him in a scarlet robe with a crown of thorns on his head and a stick in his hand as a mock king. They spat at him, beat him, and insulted him. Then they led him out to be crucified on a rocky hill just outside the city. When a person was executed, it was custom to pin above them a notice stating their crime. Pilate had written: "This is the king of the Jews."

Crucified, died...

The Roman punishment for criminals was to be nailed to a cross. Two criminals, one on either side, were executed with Jesus. One of his disciples John stood next to Jesus' mother Mary, watching. The Gospels record that from noon the whole country was covered with darkness for three hours and, when Jesus died, the earth shook and the curtain hanging in the Temple was torn in two.

... and was buried

A wealthy man named Joseph, from the town of Arimathea, asked Pilate for permission to take Jesus' body. Jesus' body was carried to a new tomb cut in the rock. There was no time for proper funeral ceremonies, as Jesus was crucified on a Friday, the day before the Sabbath day of rest. A stone door was rolled across the entrance. The religious leaders feared that Jesus' followers would take his body, so soldiers were positioned on guard outside.

Q: What were the words Jesus said on the cross?

The four Gospels record seven phrases that Jesus said and prayed while hanging on the cross.

In Matthew's and Mark's Gospels, Jesus shouts: *Eli, Eli, lema sabachthani?* which means, *My God, my God, why do you abandon me?*

In Luke's Gospel, when he is crucified, Jesus says: *Forgive them, Father! They don't know what they are doing.*

He says to the repentant criminal: *I promise you that today you will be in Paradise with me.*

He cries in a loud voice: *Father! In your hands I place my spirit!*

In John's Gospel, Jesus instructs the disciple to look after his mother: *He is your son... She is your mother.*

Jesus says, *I am thirsty* and is given wine on a sponge.

Then says: *It is finished!*

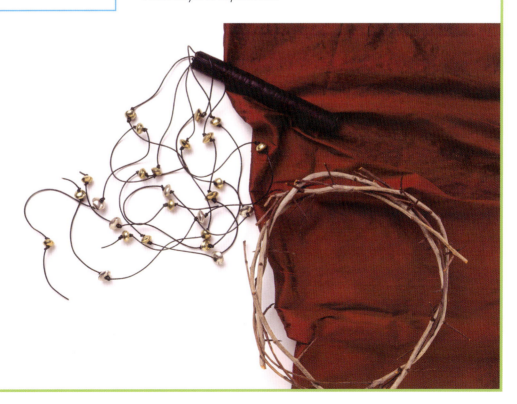

The scarlet robe, the crown of thorns, and the metal-barbed scourge are reminders of the cruelty Jesus suffered.

What happened at Jesus' RESURRECTION?

Very early on Sunday morning, a small group of women went to Jesus' tomb to complete the burial ceremonies. They found the **tomb** open and empty, and angels tell them that Jesus has **risen** and is **alive**. The Gospels each give their own **witness accounts** of Jesus appearing to his followers.

The empty tomb

The Gospel of Matthew describes how, as the women went to the tomb, there was a violent earthquake, and an angel rolled the stone away. According to Luke, they find the stone rolled away and two men in shining clothes suddenly appear. The women are told to let Jesus' disciples know that they will see Jesus. As they hurry away, the women are afraid, but also amazed and filled with joy. Peter runs to the tomb, but only the folded grave cloths are found.

Witness accounts

In Luke's Gospel, on that same day, two of Jesus' followers were walking along the road to Emmaus when a stranger appears. The stranger explains that everything that had happened to Jesus fitted with what the Scriptures said about the Messiah. They invite him to stay with them and, as the stranger breaks the bread, they recognize him as Jesus himself.

Two thousand years ago, women were not allowed or trusted to give witness in the legal courts. Yet the first witnesses to Jesus' resurrection were women.

More witnesses

The Gospel of John contains the most witness accounts of Jesus being alive. One of the women, Mary Magdalene, meets Jesus at the tomb, mistaking him to begin with for the gardener. When he says her name, she recognizes him. In the evening, the disciples are in a locked room, but Jesus stands among them. He eats and talks with them all. The disciple Thomas was not there and did not believe the others. A week later, Jesus appears and invites Thomas to see and touch the marks on his body. Afterwards, Jesus appears when the disciples are fishing on Lake Galilee, and shares breakfast with them on the shore.

Q: What is the meaning of Jesus' resurrection?

The most important and joyful day in the Christian year is Easter, when Christians celebrate their belief that Jesus rose from the dead. This return to life is called the resurrection, and convinces Christians that Jesus is God's Son, the Messiah, and his message is true: Jesus has restored the relationship between God and people, and those who belong to God's kingdom will have the hope of everlasting life.

Did you KNOW?

Christianity is the only religion that believes its founder is still alive. There is no tomb or grave for Christians to visit to show their respect for Jesus.

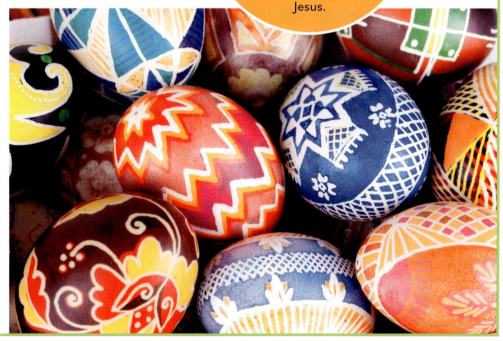

Easter eggs are a part of many Easter celebrations. They are an ancient symbol of new life.

How did NEWS about Jesus spread?

The Gospels record that Jesus gave his followers a **final instruction** to carry on spreading the message about God's kingdom. At the festival of **Pentecost**, the apostles receive the Holy Spirit. They bravely speak about Jesus and **baptize** new followers. The Christian faith begins to spread through the Roman empire, and beyond.

Christians celebrate the birth of the church on the Day of Pentecost each year.

Did you KNOW?

Christians believe that Jesus Christ is the promised king of God's kingdom. They believe that Jesus will return at the end of time. On that day of judgement, God's kingdom will be fulfilled with a new heaven and new earth.

Final instruction

After his resurrection, Jesus told his close disciples to go to people everywhere and share his teaching about God's kingdom: *Baptize them in the name of the Father, the Son and the Holy Spirit.* This is known as the "Great Commission". Jesus gave Peter special instructions to care for all believers in the same way that a shepherd takes care of sheep. He told them to wait as God would send help to strengthen them.

Ascension

After forty days, the disciples saw Jesus ascend (lifted) to heaven, and a cloud hid him from their sight. Two angels appeared beside them, saying: *This Jesus, who was taken from you into heaven, will come back in the same way that you saw him go to heaven.* They went back to Jerusalem filled with joy.

Pentecost

The Jewish festival of Pentecost was held fifty days after Passover. Jews from all over the empire again came to Jerusalem to celebrate. Luke wrote another book, the Acts of the Apostles, that records what happened. The disciples were in a locked room when they heard a noise like a strong wind and something like tongues of fire touched each of them. The disciples were filled with the Holy Spirit, rushed out into the street, and began talking about Jesus in different languages. On that day, 3,000 people were baptized as new believers, following Jesus.

The Christian faith soon began to spread across the Roman empire and beyond.

Q: Who spread the message about Jesus?

Rome

Thessalonica   Philippi

Corinth   Athens

Ephesus

Antioch

Mediterranean Sea

Jerusalem

People who heard Peter speak on the day of Pentecost returned to their countries and spread the news about Jesus.

The followers of Christ who lived in Jerusalem were given a hard time for their beliefs. Some went to other towns to spread their message elsewhere.

A disciple named Paul went on several long trips to tell people about Jesus.

GLOSSARY

Apostle: One of the twelve specially chosen followers of Jesus first sent out to spread Jesus' message.

Baptize: To mark a new beginning as a child of God, often by sprinkling over or dipping in water a new believer.

Ceremony: A celebration of an occasion, often with set words and actions.

Christ: A title based on a Greek word that means "chosen king".

Commission: An instruction given to a person or group about an important piece of work that they need to do.

Covenant: A promise or agreement between God and people, usually with a sign to mark the promise.

Disciple: A person who follows the way of life and teachings of Jesus.

Incarnation: God takes on a human form.

Messiah: A title based on a Hebrew word that means "promised king", who will save people.

Ministry: Working to show God's glory on earth.

Miracle: A wondrous deed made possible with the power of God.

Parable: A simple story with a deeper spiritual meaning.

Prayer: Words said to praise, give thanks, talk, and listen to God.

Prophecies: Predictions of what will happen in the future, often told by prophets who speak the words of God.

Resurrection: Raised from the death and come back to life.

Sabbath: A holy day of rest and focus on God.

Salvation: The rescue plan of God to bring people back to be with him.

Scriptures: Holy writings thought to be inspired by, or the actual words of, God.

Temple: A building for worship of God.

Testament: An agreement or covenant.

BIBLE REFERENCES

Jesus explained that God longs to take care of everyone, as a good parent takes care of much-loved children.

INDEX

Other titles in the KEYWORDS series:

What are Religions and Worldviews?

ISBN 978 0 7459 7968 7

What's in the Bible?

ISBN 978 0 7459 7966 3